Nelson Thornes

First published in 2007 by Cengage Learning Australia
www.cengage.com.au

This edition published under the imprint of Nelson Thornes Ltd,
Delta Place, 27 Bath Road, Cheltenham, United Kingdom, GL53 7TH

10 9 8 7 6 5 4 3
12

Text © 2007 Cengage Learning Australia Pty Ltd ABN 14058280149
(incorporated in Victoria)
Illustrations © 2007 Cengage Learning Australia Pty Ltd ABN 14058280149
(incorporated in Victoria)

The right of Julia Wall to be identified as author of this work has been asserted by him/her in accordance with the Copyright, Designs and Patents Act 1988

All rights reserved. No part of this publication may be reproduced or transmitted in any form or by any means, electronic or mechanical, including photocopy, recording or any information storage and retrieval system, without permission in writing from the publisher or under licence from the Copyright Licensing Agency Limited, of 90 Tottenham Court Road, London W1T 4LP.

Any person who commits any unauthorised act in relation to this publication may be liable to criminal prosecution and civil claims for damages.

Marty and the Magazine
ISBN 978-1-4085-0112-2

Story by Julia Wall
Illustrations by Karen Oppatt
Edited by Cameron Macintosh
Designed by Vonda Pestana
Series Design by James Lowe
Production Controller Emma Hayes
Audio recordings by Juliet Hill, Picture Start
Spoken by Matthew King and Abbe Holmes
Printed in China by 1010 Printing International Ltd

Website www.nelsonthornes.com

Marty and the Magazine

Julia Wall — *Karen Oppatt*

Contents

Chapter 1 Mr Mancini's Music Shop 4
Chapter 2 "It's Marty's!" 12
Chapter 3 Keeping the Magazine 18
Chapter 4 Something Had Changed 21

Chapter 1

MR MANCINI'S MUSIC SHOP

Joe and I liked
Mr Mancini's music shop.
It had the best CDs
and music magazines.
We hung out there most Fridays
after school.

One Friday, I chose a CD
that I'd been saving for
and went to pay for it.
The woman in front of me
was talking to Mr Mancini.
He was giving one of his big,
hearty laughs.

I looked in the mirror
that was up behind Mr Mancini.
That's when I saw Joe
pick up a music magazine –
then look around
and put it in his jacket.

My heart was going so fast
that I felt sick.
Mr Mancini was saying goodbye
to the woman,
so he didn't see a thing.

Marty and the Magazine

My hand was shaking as I paid for my CD.

"Hey, Marty," Mr Mancini said. "What's the matter? You look like you've seen a ghost!"

Joe came up behind me as Mr Mancini gave another one of his big, hearty laughs.

Marty and the Magazine

"You boys have a good day!" he called after us as we left.

I felt so bad that I didn't turn around and give him a wave.

When we were outside on the street,
Joe pulled the magazine
out of his jacket.
"Look what I got!" he said.

"IT'S MARTY'S!"

"I know," I said,
looking at the magazine.
"I saw you take it, in the mirror."

"Really?
I hope no one else saw me."
Joe started looking at the magazine.
"This one has some really cool reviews,"
he said.

I was about to say something when we ran into Joe's mum.

"Where did you get that magazine from, Joe?" she asked.

Marty and the Magazine

"It's Marty's," said Joe, quickly.
"I was just taking a look."
He gave me the magazine.

"Is that so?" asked Joe's mum.

I looked at Joe,
and I looked at his mum.
My heart started going fast again.

"Yes," I said.
"I bought it from Mr Mancini's."

I could tell that Joe's mum believed me.

"Well, I'm off to get some pizza," she said.
"You boys head on home now."

Joe and I nodded as she got into her car.

"Thanks, Marty," said Joe.
"You really saved me."

I didn't say anything.

"Can I have the magazine back?" he asked.

KEEPING THE MAGAZINE

"I think I'll keep it for a while," I said, looking at Joe.
"You don't want your mum finding it."
I put it in my jacket.

"Okay," said Joe, but I could tell he wasn't happy.

"How about some basketball tomorrow?" he asked.

"Maybe," I said.
"I'll call you later tonight, if I'm free."

That night, I didn't call.
Instead, I played around
on my computer, and felt down.
Joe had been my friend
since we were small,
but now something had changed.

SOMETHING HAD CHANGED

On Saturday, I went back
to Mr Mancini's music shop
with the magazine in my jacket.

Mr Mancini saw me and gave one of his big, hearty laughs.

"Back so soon?" he asked.

"Just looking, Mr Mancini," I said.
I slipped the magazine out of my jacket and back onto the shelf.

The next time I saw Joe
was on Monday at school.

"Hi," he said.
I said 'hi' back, but I didn't feel like
I was talking to the Joe
I used to hang out with
at Mr Mancini's music shop.
I felt like I was talking to someone
I didn't know –
someone who was no longer my friend.